THE ANCIENT GREEKS

THE ANCIENT GREEKS
In The Land of the Gods

BY SOPHIE DESCAMPS-LEQUIME
AND DENISE VERNEREY

Illustrations by Annie-Claude Martin

Translated by Mary Kae LaRose

PEOPLES OF THE PAST

The Millbrook Press
Brookfield, Connecticut

Library of Congress Cataloging-in-Publication Data

Descamps-Lequime, Sophia.
[Au pays des dieux. English]
The ancient Greeks : in the land of the Gods / by Sophie Descamps-
Lequime and Denise Vernerey : illustrated by Annie-Claude Martin ;
translated by Mary Kae LaRose.
p.   cm.—(Peoples of the past)
Translation of: : Au pays des dieux.
Includes bibliographical references and index.
Summary: Details the clothing, eating habits, political structure,
culture, and other aspects of daily life in ancient Greece.
ISBN 1-56294-069-4
1. Greece—Civilization—To 146 B.C.—Juvenile literature.
[1. Greece—Civilization—To 146 B.C.]   I. Vernerey, Denise,
II. Martin, Annie Claude, il.   III. Title.   IV. Series; Peoples of
the past (Brookfield, Conn.)
DF77.D47   1992
938—dc20   91-35941   CIP   AC

CONTENTS

INTRODUCTION

The Greeks lived in a land peopled by gods. They believed that a network of powerful beings controlled the course of their lives. Today, we tend to look at these religious beliefs as mythology, fascinating and informative, but fiction nonetheless. And yet, when we stop to ponder the tremendous achievements of the Greeks, it is easy to believe that they were in touch with a higher power.

The Greeks were unusually curious about themselves and the world. They had a lively sense of adventure and the desire to seek out not only the truth but the most beautiful way to express this truth to others.

These people of the past have left us many messages about who they were—in their writings and in the artifacts that modern archeologists have dug from the ground. But it is not necessary to look back to learn about the Greeks. Evidence of their achievement is all around us. Language, philosophy, art, architecture, science, democracy—these cornerstones of our Western world were laid in the fertile imaginations of the ancient Greeks.

A look at the time line on the following pages will help to orient you. Greek civilization lasted for about two thousand years Before Christ (B.C.). Western civilization has continued to flourish for about the same length of time in the years Anno Domini (A.D.), Latin for in the year of the Lord.

This book will lead you to imagine what it was like to live as a Greek in the fifth century B.C. It will also tell you about the accomplishments of some of the most famous citizens of Greece.

It was in this period that Socrates lived, a philosopher whose ideas continue to shape our world. Pericles ruled Athens in a revolutionary way that gave power to the citizens themselves—giving birth to what we now call democracy. The playrights Aeschylus, Sophocles, and Euripides produced dramas upon which our modern plays are based. This was the peak of Greek civilization—its Golden Age.

A WALK THROUGH GREEK HISTORY

NEOLITHIC PERIOD

Circa (about) 4000
Nomads settle in Greece and towns begin to develop.

BRONZE AGE

3200
2000   First Greek-speaking people arrive in Greece.
1700   The island of Crete, which has not been invaded by Greek-speaking people,
        dominates the Aegean Islands.
1600
1400   Rise of Mycenaean culture on the Peloponnese.

DARK AGES   *(1200–900 B.C.)*

1200   Invasions. Decline of Mycenaean civilization.
1184   Siege of Troy.
1050

GEOMETRIC PERIOD   *(900–720 B.C.)*

900
776   First Olympic Games
750   Greeks begin to found such colonies in the West as Syracuse, Marseilles,
       and Tarantum.

ORIENTALIZING PERIOD   *(720–620 B.C.)*

700
660   Greek cities are governed by tyrants.
650

IRON AGE

THE ARCHAIC PERIOD   *(620–480 B.C.)*

592   Solon begins to reform the Athenian political system.
550   Peisistratus the tyrant and his sons seize power in Athens.
510   End of tyranny. Cleisthenes introduces political reforms that lead to the birth
       of democracy in Athens.
499   Conflicts with the Persian Empire begin.
490   Athenian victory over the Persians at Marathon.

First marble sculptures are found in the Cyclades.

Cycladic "idol," c. 2500 B.C.

Fresco from the Palace of Knossos on Crete, *"The Parisian"*

Gold Mycenean funeral mask

Mycenaeans speak Greek. Their writing, Linear B, has been deciphered by modern scholars.

Writing disappears.

City-states are born.
Greek alphabet is created.

Greek art is influenced by the Orient.

Black figure pottery begins to appear.

First traces of monumental sculpture appear in the work of Daedalus.

Geometric amphora (2-handled jug), c. 750 B.C.

Aryballos (perfume flask).

Daedalic sculpture, c. 640 B.C.

Designs for Ionic and Doric Order temples.
Height of black figure pottery.
Red figure pottery develop.

"Bilingual Amphora" uses both black and red styles.

First representation of young male nude, or kouros, and young draped maiden, or kore.

Kore, c. 530 B.C.

Kouros, c. 500 B.C.

CLASSICAL AGE *(480–323 B.C.)*

480 Persians destroy the Athenian Acropolis.

479 Persians are repelled from Greece at the Battle of Plataea.

454 Athens dominates the Greek city-states.

448 Pericles is elected strategos, or commander of the Athenian army.

431 Sparta invades Athens. The Peloponnesian War begins.

404 Spartan victory over Athens.

399 Socrates is condemned to death.

356 Philip II becomes king of Macedonia.

338 Philip II defeats the Hellenic League at the Battle of Chaeronea.
Decline of Greek city-states.

336 Philip II is assassinated.
His son, Alexander the Great, succeeds him to the throne.
Alexander leads military campaigns in Asia.

332 Alexander dies.

HELLENISTIC PERIOD *(323–31 B.C.)*

321 Alexander's generals divide the empire between them.
Founding of the Hellenistic kingdoms.
Rise of Roman power.

272 Romans sack Tarantum.

197 Romans defeat the Macedonians.

146 Romans take Corinth and impose Roman rule on Greece and Macedonia.

86 Sulla and the Romans sack Athens.

31 Battle of Actium. Cleopatra is defeated and Rome wins Egypt, the last independent Hellenistic kingdom.

First traces of the severe style in sculpture.

Transition from the severe style to classicism.

Pericles orders that the building of the Acropolis begin.

Polyclitus refines techniques to represent the human body.

Discus Thrower of Myron, c. 450 B.C.

Sophocles's Antigone.

Euripides's Medea.

Aristophanes's Peace.

First stone theaters are built.

Phidias's Athena Parthenos, the Parthenon, c. 438 B.C.

Plato founds the Academy in Athens.

Aphrodite of Cnidus, c. 350 B.C.

Praxiteles sculpts the first female nude.

Aristotle opens his school of philosophy, the Lyceum.

Lysippus is the official portraitist at Alexander's court.

Growth of many artistic centers.

Child with a Goose

First representations of early childhood.

Psyche of Antioch c. 300 B.C.

Nike of Samothrace, c. 190 B.C.

Representation of the city-state of Antioch.

Venus de Milo, c. 100 B.C.

THE ANCIENT GREEK WORLD

In the fifth century B.C., Greece was a much larger country than it is today. Greek civilization spread north into southern Russia, west across the sea to Italy, south to Egypt, and east into the heart of Asia Minor.

The harsh climate and poor soil on the mountain-covered mainland led the Greeks to search out other, more fertile lands for the food and supplies they needed.

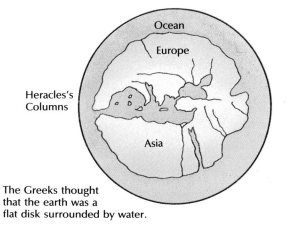

The Greeks thought that the earth was a flat disk surrounded by water.

Greek trading posts and colonies hugged the coasts of the Mediterranean, Aegean, and Black seas. Greek ships exported their olive oil, wine, and pottery to other countries in exchange for a great variety of goods.

From the lands surrounding the Black Sea came grain. The coasts of Asia Minor and Europe were sources for the copper and tin that the Greeks turned into weapons and armor. Food—dates, nuts, fish, beef, spices—came from as far away as central Asia Minor and northern Italy. From Egypt came papyrus reeds to make writing paper, and from lands north of the Aegean came the timber to build their fleets of ships.

The ancient Greeks used the Aegean Sea as their private roadway. The islands of Crete, the Cyclades, and the Sporades were mere stopping points along the way to their trading posts.

Greek colonists founded the cities of Cyrene and Naucratis in Libya and Egypt and the cities of Massalia and Thelines on the southern coast of France. (These later became the French cities of Marseilles and Arles.) There were so many colonies in southern Italy and Sicily that they were often called Magna Graecia, or Great Greece.

And yet, the Greeks did not often mix with the inhabitants of these foreign lands. Anyone who didn't speak their language was simply called a "barbarian."

Many Greeks did not know that their world was so vast. They spent their lives within the boundaries of their own city-state, which included a town and surrounding villages and farmlands. There were more than three hundred of these independent regions.

Land of Yellow Blossoms

Sparta was located in a fertile plain filled with grape vines and olive trees.
It grew out of a small settlement built around a shrine dedicated to the goddess Artemis. Sparta's name most likely came from a flowering shrub called the Spanish broom (Spartivm ivnceum) that was abundant in the region.

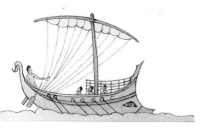

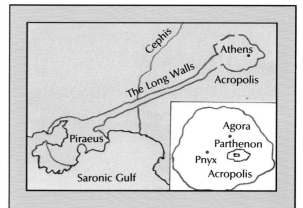

Even though these city-states often quarreled and sometimes even fought with one another—as in the case of Athens and Sparta—people living in these many different areas shared a common culture. They all spoke dialects of the Greek language, believed in the same gods, and had many customs in common. In short, even though the city-states of Greece never united into a single nation, their inhabitants were definitely Greeks.

Let's look now at what it was like to grow up as a Greek about 2,500 years ago.

The Athenian City-State

Athens was in a pleasant place located near the sea. The city-state was large and included a port called Piraeus. A 4-mile (6-km) road lined with The Long Walls connected the port to the heart of the city. The city itself was a fortress protected by solid walls. In the center of Athens was the Acropolis, a tall, rocky hill dedicated to the city's patron goddess and protector Athena.

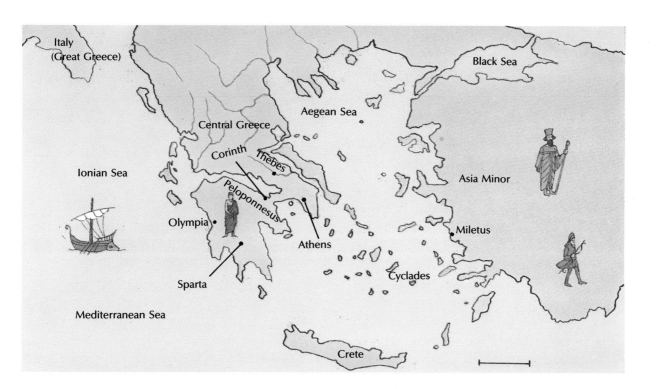

GROWING UP IN GREECE

" A son is always kept and raised into adulthood, even if his family is poor. A daughter is left to die, even one born of a rich family," wrote Posidippus, a comic poet. Certainly he exaggerated. But it was true that a boy in ancient Greece had a better chance of living than a girl. The birth of a healthy baby, especially if it was a boy, was cause for celebration in wealthy families. On the other hand, poor families worried that another mouth to feed would reduce them to even worse poverty. Fathers had the right to abandon their newborn infants outdoors. Children who were exposed in this way would die if nobody took them in. Sometimes other people adopted these unwanted babies and brought them up to be their slaves.

GREEK CHILDHOOD

Until the age of seven, children lived in the women's quarters with their mothers. They were nursed by their mothers or hired nurses. They slept in wicker baskets or wooden cradles and fell asleep to the sound of lullabies.

In warlike Sparta, babies were not wrapped in blankets but were left to wriggle about as they pleased. This was believed to make them strong and healthy. The Athenians, who looked at Sparta's military ways with fear and scorn, respected the Spartans' expertise in raising children. They often hired Spartan nurses to raise their own babies.

The philosopher Aristotle advised: "It is important that children be kept busy so that they won't break things inside the house."

Plato, another philosopher, spoke in favor of opening "children's parks filled with educational games."

Greek boys and girls didn't need to be told to play games. They played many different kinds on their own. They played with balls and knuckle bones, and they had lots of toys: miniature chariots, rattles, yo-yos, rocking horses, and earthenware dolls and animals. They liked to play with pets, too,

especially dogs. They would also play with ducks, quail, mice, weasels, and even grass-hoppers.

At around age seven, boys and girls went their separate ways. The boys were sent to school each morning while the girls for the most part stayed home.

SPARTAN SCHOOLS

The schools of the city-states varied. In Sparta, education was extremely severe. As soon as children turned seven, the city-state took charge of their schooling. They were sent off to military camps.

Until age fourteen, Spartan students learned only the basics of reading and writing. The government wanted to develop the students' physical abilities more than anything else. The young school boys had their heads shaved, and they wore little clothing and no shoes. They slept on rough beds made of reeds and were not allowed to use covers. Boys were purposely fed too little to encourage them to steal food. All this training was aimed at preparing the boys for the time when the region would go to war.

Even girls received physical education and competed in sporting events, which other

A Famous Author

Homer, who lived in the eighth century B.C., *is credited with two epic poems about Greece. The Iliad describes the Greek expedition to the city of Troy, and the Odyssey tells about the return of Ulysses from the war that was fought there. Young Greeks knew the works of Homer quite well and memorized long passages from the Iliad and the Odyssesy.*

ATHENIAN SCHOOLS

Unlike Sparta, the city-state of Athens did not take charge of its young children. A child's education was left up to the father. At dawn, young Athenians left home for the residence of their private schoolmaster. Boys from wealthy families were accompanied by slaves called *pedagogues* who looked after them and carried their books and pencils. A special teacher called a *grammatist* taught them reading and writing for three or four years. Sometimes the teacher unrolled a long papyrus scroll and asked the students to re-cite lines from a well-known writer such as Homer or Hesiod.

The grammatist sat on a straight-backed chair while the pedagogue and student sat on stools. There were no tables. Students wrote on hard, wax-covered tablets that they balanced on their knees. The teacher made light marks on the tablet that the student then traced with the pointed end of his stylus, a wooden writing instrument. A cross-shaped ruler helped the students keep the letters in a straight line.

Greeks found shocking. But the Spartans wanted their women to be strong so that they would give birth to healthy children.

When young Spartan men turned twenty, they were admitted to the ranks of "accom-plished men" and taught how to use weapons and to serve in military formations.

A Love of Music

Musical training was much valued in Greece. The music teacher sat down when he taught his student to play the kithara; he stood before his student when teaching him the double flute. The student listened hard and then tried to imitate his master's music.

Themistocles, an important Athenian statesman, regretted that he had never learned to play music, the mark of a cultivated man.

Athenian students learned the four mathematical operations of addition, subtraction, multiplication, and division. They also learned to work with fractions.

The Greeks spent a lot of time and energy on physical education. Twelve-year-old boys were sent to sports facilities where they were coached by a *paidotribe,* who specialized in adolescent athletic training. This coach wore a purple cloak and leaned on a long, forked cane when he supervised the physical education classes.

The children of wealthy parents learned to ride horseback. And a person was not considered to be truly educated unless he had learned to wrestle, use a bow and sling, and swim. Greeks had a saying for someone who they thought was not very smart: "He doesn't even know how to read or swim!"

A WOMAN'S LOT

Greeks had a saying about how girls ought to behave: "See little, hear little, and ask no more questions than are absolutely necessary."

Young Greek girls did not go to school. They mastered only the basics of reading, math, and music and learned how to keep house in the company of their mothers, relatives, and servants. Girls were taught to be good mistresses of their homes. They were not supposed to become clever and cultivated women.

A Greek joke shows that this was indeed the case. One person asks, "Do you know anybody with whom you have had fewer conversations than your wife?" Another person replies, "I can think of nobody with whom I speak less."

Athenian girls and women from wealthy families almost never left home. They ventured outdoors only to attend religious festivals and family celebrations such as a birth or a funeral. Their slaves did all of the household shopping.

Poor women had no choice but to go out into the streets. They had to make a living. But such women were not thought well of. Even the mother of the poet Euripides was scorned by her neighbors for her daily outing to the market where she would sell the parsley she had grown in her garden.

Within their own homes respectable women were confined to special quarters called the *gynaeceum*. The lady of the house ruled over this part of her home and supervised the work of the slaves. Husbands had a saying, though, to keep their wives in line: "Do not spend in one month's time the money that should last all year long."

Some women were not required to live by this rigid social code. The laws that governed the behavior of Athenian women did not apply to women who were not originally from Athens. For example, Sappho, a noblewoman from the island of Lesbos, wrote fine poetry. And Aspasia, who came from Miletus on the coast of Asia Minor, became Pericles' special companion. Through her clever wit and finely tuned intelligence she gained the confidence of this great Athenian statesman. Her foreign origin allowed her to live more freely than Athenian women.

AN ATHENIAN BRIDE

Greek girls did not usually meet the husbands that their fathers had chosen for them until their wedding day. They had no say in the matter. Marriages were seen as alliances between families, and such decisions were left to the fathers and future husbands.

Different Worlds

Young Greek girls almost never left the gynaeceum. They rarely saw their fathers and brothers, who lived in separate quarters. When their fathers invited guests home, neither the girls nor their mother was invited to the party.

Girls married when they were about fifteen years old, while the bridegroom was often at least thirty. The girls' father offered the bridegroom a sum of money and goods called a dowry. Her husband would control these funds, and if he should die, both the woman and her dowry were returned to her father.

The day before her wedding, a girl bathed in water from a sacred spring. The water was poured from a vase called a *loutrophorus*. She then presented her childhood toys and a lock of hair to Artemis, the goddess of the moon and the hunt.

The following poem tells us what a young girl named Timareta offered as a symbol of her entry into the adult world of married life:

The Marriage Month

Weddings usually took place in January. This month, which was called Gamelion, *was dedicated to Hera, the goddess of marriage. The Greek word for marriage was* gamos.

young people who died before reaching marriageable age had special tombs. Their marble tombstones were engraved with the image of the loutrophourus, the vase that would have purified them on the day before their wedding.

SPARTAN WEDDINGS

Spartan weddings were a reflection of a very different way of life. Athenian women may have been denied the rights of a citizen but they were also carefully protected. This was not the case for a woman born and raised in Sparta.

There, women conditioned themselves through sports such as running and wrestling to be warriors in the battle of childbirth. Those who were well armed with a strong, muscular physique were most likely to survive.

"The day of her wedding Timareta gave Artemis her tambourines, her ball, and her hairnet. To Artemis she also gave as was appropriate, her dolls and all their clothing."

The bride wore a white robe and a crown and veil to the wedding banquet, which was held in her father's house. In the evening after the party the bride and groom rode in a chariot—or in a cart if the families were poor—led by a joyous procession to the husband's house.

The groom's mother welcomed them to the house. The bride was then carried over the threshold and invited to join in the life of her new family.

Of course, there were some people who never married. Single men and women and

Spartan weddings, like Spartan childbirth, were not romanticized. The writer Plutarch described Spartan weddings as a test for young girls rather than as a celebration.

She had no pretty dress; nor was there a party or procession. Rather, the couple met briefly and in private. Then, the man went back to sleep with his friends.

Afterward, the newlyweds were only allowed to see each other in secret. It was only when the husband reached the age of thirty that he was permitted to leave his comrades and live in the same house as his wife. Marriage was meant only to produce children, not to offer a husband the comfort of a loving wife.

DRESSING IN STYLE

Greek clothing was simple and free-flowing. Even though the social codes for men and women were very distinct, the difference between their ways of dressing was more a matter of style than anything else.

The materials used in different periods by different classes of people did vary, though. Most clothes were made of wool or linen until the Greeks began importing cotton from India in the fifth century B.C. In the following century, the island of Kos began to produce silk, a luxurious material that only the wealthy could afford.

Greek garments had no definite shape. Tunics and cloaks were formed by draping simple rectangles of cloth around the body with belts, hooks, buttons, or brooches. Garments could be returned to their rectangular shape at any moment simply by releasing the belts and fasteners.

A story circulated in ancient Greece about a well-known miser named Phocion who was able to save money because of the simplicity of Greek fashion. He and his wife shared a single piece of clothing! When Phocion wrapped the rectangle of woolen cloth around his body, it served as a cloak. When his wife attached it to her shoulders and tied a belt around her waist, it turned into a tunic. The husband and wife took turns going out of the house. And then, at night, all Phocion had to do was free the cloth from its fasteners to produce a wool blanket for their bed!

Many different styles of dress could be created in just a few moments from a rectangle of cloth. With one piece of wool women could make a tunic or twelve different styles of cloaks.

Tunics—or *peplos,* as they were called in Greek—were made by folding the fabric lengthwise and then folding back a flap of the fabric. The tunic was then fastened on both sides of the neck with two long pins or

Little Girls' Fashions

The young girls often wore beltless peplos. The material hung down freely, and the folds in the fabric shifted as the girls moved and played.

was expected to grow into it. In the meantime, she had to find a way to make a tunic that she wouldn't trip on. How did she do it? She pulled the fabric above her belt so that it wouldn't drag on the ground. The puffy, folded gathers around her waist hid the surplus cloth.

metal brooches called *fibulae*. The hanging fabric was then pulled in at the waist with a belt.

Even this simple style could be varied. The flap could be short or reach to mid-thigh. The belt could be placed under a short flap or over a long one.

A teenage girl might be given a piece of cloth that must last her into adulthood. The fabric she received might be as much as three yards long and two yards wide. She

In Cold Weather

Peplos didn't have sleeves. In the regions where winters were cold, Greek women wrapped their arms in the folds of fabric that draped from their shoulders. If they had thrown a wool cloak over their shoulders, they could warm their hands inside its folds as well.

Cloaks called *himations* were made with a second rectangle of wool. Both men and women wore them. They draped the fabric

24

across their shoulders and let it hang down their backs. Sometimes they carried it over their arms like a shawl. Most often, they wrapped it around their body, carefully draping one end of it over their left shoulder. In chilly weather they might make a snugly hooded coat. Men sometimes leaned on long sticks that held the many folds of fabric in place under their arms.

Hairstyles

Women tied back their hair with cloth headbands called cecryphalaes *that wrapped all the way around their head. Or sometimes they simply pulled up the flap from their peplos to cover their hair.*

creases in it, imagine how difficult it was to make the many vertical pleats of the elegant chiton. Women made finger pleats by sliding the fabric through their fingers, pinching it as they went along.

Chiton sleeves were made by fastening together the edges of the fabric from the

The *chiton* was an especially popular tunic among women. Its delicate pleats of transparent linen shimmered in the light. But the Greeks didn't have irons! Clothing was simply folded and stored in large chests. Since this tended to leave the fabric with horizontal

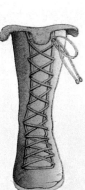

Footgear

Greeks wore shoes only when they went outdoors. Everybody wore thin-strapped sandals. For women, there were also ankle boots made of soft leather; young men wore tall, heavy boots with laces. Greek soldiers often went barefoot.

shoulders to the wrists. The fabric pulled away from each clasp, creating lovely, oval-shaped openings all along the arms.

Bright colors—red, yellow, violet, and blue—were popular. Greeks were sensitive to subtle shades of color, too. They distinguished, for example, between forest green, apple green, mint green, and olive green. All of their cloth was woven at home. Wool was always dyed, but linen was left white. Young

women wore soft-colored woolen peplos over white linen chitons.

Young men often wore thigh-length tunics. When they went hunting or riding, they might also drape a *chlamys,* or short cloak, over one shoulder. Only craftsmen and slaves wore loincloths.

Short Chitons

When young women wanted to move around more easily than they could in their long robes, they shortened their tunics by simply pulling the fabric up through their belts. The new layer of billowing folds was held in place at the waist by a second belt.

WAYS OF LIFE

Ordinary Greek homes had only two or three rooms and were so small that their doors had to open to the outside. Before going out, Greeks knocked on the door to avoid bumping into passersby making their way up the steep, twisting street.

In Athens the streets zigzagged in an irregular grid that made allowance for the steepness of the terrain. In other cities, however,

streets crossed at right angles. It was an architect from Miletus named Hippodamus who designed the checkerboard pattern for the streets of Piraeus, the port of Athens.

In poor homes there were no kitchens. All the cooking was done outside over a campfire so that the house didn't fill with smoke. Many homes didn't have chimneys but had small vents in the ceiling instead. In the winter when fires had to be built indoors for warmth, Greeks removed tiles from the roof and broke several holes at the top of the walls to let the smoke out.

In most parts of the city houses were made of wood, mud bricks, or stones stuck together with mortar. Thieves were called "wall-diggers" because they would break holes in the walls of the houses to steal valuable objects inside.

Expensive homes had walls that were about 1 foot (30.5 centimeters) thick. The lower part of the wall was made of stone and the

Homeless

If a tenant couldn't pay the rent on time, the landlord might remove the door from the house, take away the roof tiles, or even block the tenant's access to the well. Then this person would join the crowd of homeless people who found refuge in the warmth of the public baths.

room where men ate and entertained their friends, called the *andron,* opened onto the courtyard. The family dining room, or *oikos,* was often next to the kitchen and bathroom, so that all of these rooms could be heated at the same time. The master bedroom, the *gynaeceum* (the section reserved for the women), and the cubby holes where slaves slept were on the second floor.

upper part was brick. There were some truly splendid Greek residences. Excavators at Olynthus have reconstructed the floor plan of about one hundred houses from the fourth century B.C. The floor plans of two of these elegant homes are shown below.

The main rooms were luxuriously decorated with stone mosaics (pictures) and were typically located in the northern part of the house. They opened onto a courtyard that was attached to a portico, or columned entranceway, called a *pastas.* The living room, or *aule,* was always cool and bright. The

Scandalous Luxury

In the fifth century B.C., Greeks believed that luxury should be reserved only for the gods. An Athenian statesman named Alcibiades owned such a splendid house that it offended his neighbors. It was rumored that he had locked a well-known painter named Agatharcos in his house until he had painted frescoes on all the walls.

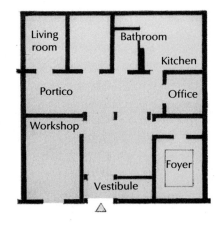
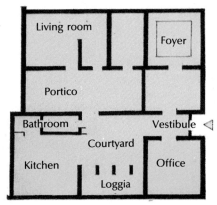

EATING, DRINKING, AND MAKING MERRY

The Greeks didn't have watches. They measured time with sundials and water clocks called *clepsydrae*. The rhythm of their days, though, was set by their meals.

Breakfast was at sunrise. Greeks ate chunks of bread dipped in wine along with some dates and figs. Their midday meal was even smaller than this. They might eat only a bit of bread with some cheese, olives, or figs. A late afternoon snack helped them make it to the main meal at the day's end. This might

consist of a thick porridge, or stew, made from barley and an assortment of vegetables. And always, there was bread.

Homer called the Greeks "flour eaters" because of the large quantity of bread they ate. They liked wheat and barley cereals, which they saw as gifts from the kind gods. Greeks of the fifth century B.C. usually bought a flat loaf of barley bread called *maza* or a round loaf of wheat bread called *artos* everyday. There were lots of different breads to choose from: milk bread, rye bread, wheaten bread, farmhouse bread, brown bread, braided bread, and square bread. However, Athenian soil could only feed one fourth of the pop-

ulation. So, the import of wheat was a major concern of Athenian politicians.

The Boeotians, who lived northwest of the Athenians, had a reputation for being big eaters and drinkers, but most Greeks made do with very little. Spartan men, for example, ate a simple daily meal of black gruel, or stew, seasoned with bacon, blood, vinegar, and honey. A typical meal for a Greek peasant was liquid barley porridge seasoned with mint. This was called *kykeion*.

Meat was expensive, and so ordinary Greeks only tasted it on the days when bulls, sheep, goats, or lambs were sacrificed to the gods as a way of asking for a special favor. Only wealthy Greeks could afford to enjoy roast beef, bean cakes, and boiled peas at their evening meal.

Recipes

The chef Epaenite advised that meats be stuffed with honey and that an intestine mixture be seasoned with vinegar and onions. He fried wild guinea hens and dormice in a honey-vinegar sauce.

However, there was much game to be hunted in the Greek countryside—pheasant, partridge, quail, and wild guinea hens. Owls, though, were never killed because they were the bird of Athena, the daughter of Zeus and the goddess of wisdom. The Greeks did hunt just about everything else: wild boars, bear, deer, foxes, weasels, hares, moles, cats, porcupines, and hedgehogs all went into the stew pot.

Fish was within everybody's budget. While only the people living in the countryside and the wealthy could eat meat on a regular basis, fishermen caught gilt-heads, mullets, turbot, and tuna all along the coast. Greeks especially liked salted tuna marinated in oil. Archestratis, a famous chef from Sicily, recommended that fish be wrapped in fig leaves and cooked in the fire's ashes.

The Greeks often ate peas, navy beans, and lentils. Together with a bit of bread, these vegetables made up the poor man's diet. Green vegetables such as green beans, lettuce, and cabbage were rare and expensive. Greeks began cultivating mushrooms in the fifth century B.C. Because mushrooms were abundant during the rainy season, Greeks thought it was thunder that caused them to appear.

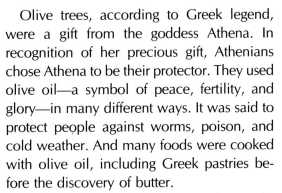

cakes and pies. They made cheesecakes, honey pies, and dried fig cakes. *Plakon* was a special cake made with flour, fresh cream, and honey. Honey was an ingredient in almost all dessert recipes. The honey that came from the Hymettus mountains near Athens was particularly famous. It was used to sweeten wild grapeleaf jam, rose-petal cakes, and spice bread.

Water was the beverage Greeks drank the

Olive trees, according to Greek legend, were a gift from the goddess Athena. In recognition of her precious gift, Athenians chose Athena to be their protector. They used olive oil—a symbol of peace, fertility, and glory—in many different ways. It was said to protect people against worms, poison, and cold weather. And many foods were cooked with olive oil, including Greek pastries before the discovery of butter.

Desserts often followed a meal. Greeks liked fresh fruits such as apples, prunes, apricots, cherries, and dates. They also liked figs, which were the fruit of Dionysus, the god of wine. In the fifth century B.C. melons were very expensive because they had to be imported from Egypt.

At that time there weren't any specialized cake bakers, but the bakers who made bread sold at least twenty-four different kinds of

most. Some preferred milk, especially goat's milk, with their meals. Others liked *hydromel,* or mead, an alcoholic drink made with water and fermented honey.

Wine was thick and heavy. It was flavored with honey and special seasonings. Greeks filtered their wine and diluted it with water before drinking it. This was an expensive beverage that only the rich could afford.

Banquets were a common form of relaxation—among men, that is. Sometimes everyone brought something along; more often, though, one man invited his friends to his home and served them dinner.

Slaves met the guests at the door. Since Greeks ate lying down, it was important that the slaves wash the guests' feet before leading them into the dining room. The food was laid out on small tables, which were placed near each couch. After washing their hands, Greeks drank flavored wine as an aperitif—that is, to stimulate the appetite. A large pottery wine goblet was passed from hand to hand before the meal began.

Ancient Greeks didn't have forks or napkins. They wiped their hands on pieces of bread that they then tossed to their dogs. They ate stew and porridge with spoons, and they cut their meat with knives. Plates, serving platters, and bowls were made of wood, clay, or metal. Slaves offered the guests several different dishes at each course.

The second part of the banquet, called the *symposium,* was for drinking and talking. Everyone drank wine that had been mixed with water in a large vase called a *krater.* After making a toast to Dionysus and chanting some hymns, the guests chose a banquet king. This man decided how much water would be added to the wine and how many goblets of wine each guest would drink. During the course of the symposium each guest was toasted by his friends.

Ready, Aim . . .

Cottabos *was a game commonly played at Greek banquets. The trick was to spin a cup with a few drops of wine in it so that the wine flew out and into a nearby vase. The most skilled wine spinner won a prize—apples, eggs, cakes, sandals, or perhaps a ball.*

TIME OFF!

Greeks didn't go away on trips the way we do. However, their work was often interrupted by religious festivals or city-state holidays. Greeks, who believed that many gods ruled over the heavens and earth, devoted a total of two months out of the year to the worship of their gods. This meant that parents and children had a full two months off. In February, there were so many holidays that Phocion (the man who shared his clothing with his wife) didn't send his sons to school at all. According to the story, he said it was much too expensive to pay a full month of tuition for so few days in school!

THE YEARLY CALENDAR
OF FESTIVITIES

Here is a nine-month Greek calendar listing all the important holidays. The Greek year began in July/August, the month of Hecatombaion.

HECATOMBAION *(July/August)*
Cronia (harvest festival)
Panathenaea (festival in honor of Athena)

BOEDROMION *(August/September)*
Great mysteries of Eleusis (11 days)

PYANOPSION *(October/November)*
Apatouries (festival in honor of Athena and Zeus)
Pyanepsies (Apollo)
Thesmophories (Demeter)
Oschophories (Dionysus and Athena)
Khalkeia (Athena and Hephaestus)

POSEIDEION *(December/January)*
Italoa (Demeter and Dionysus)
Rural Dionysian festival

GAMELION *(January/February)*
Lenaea (festival in honor of Dionysus)

ANTHESTERION *(February/March)*
Anthesteries (festivals in honor of Dionysus and the dead)
Minor mysteries of Eleusis
Diasies (festival in honor of Zeus)
Chloia (Demeter)

ELAPHEBOLION *(March/April)*
Procharisteria (Athena)
Great Dionysia (6 days)

THARGELION *(May/June)*
Thargelies (Apollo or Demeter)
Thalysies (Demeter and Cora)

SCIROPHORION *(June/July)*
Skira (Demeter and Cora)
Dipolies-Bouphonies (Zeus)
Arretophoria (Athena and Aphrodite)

Athena, goddess of wisdom and war; Demeter, goddess of the earth and harvests; Zeus, the ruler of the gods and the heavens; and Dionysus, god of wine, were all very important gods and goddesses. They were celebrated several times during the year.

WOMEN JOIN IN

Some holidays were specifically for women. For example, married women from good families participated in the Thesmophories in honor of Demeter, the goddess of the earth and fertility. In Athens this festival, which lasted from the ninth to the thirteenth day of Pyanopsion, was particularly important.

During the first two days of the festival, a procession made its way toward the temple of Demeter on Cape Kolias. On the fourth day, after the women had returned to Athens, they observed a day of mourning and fasting. On the festival's final day there was a banquet at which everybody danced. The holiday closed with the sacrifice of an animal.

The following month, during Poseideion, women celebrated Demeter again. This time, however, during the festival of Italoa they also celebrated Dionysus, the god of wine and vegetation.

THE PANATHENAIC FESTIVAL

The most important Athenian holiday was the great Panathenaic procession, which could almost be seen as a national Greek holiday. This spectacular festival in honor of Athena took place every fourth year. A long procession wound its way up to the Acropolis.

Nine months before the festival began, young women from respected Athenian families were chosen to serve as *ergastinae*, or

The Battle of the Gods

A gigantomachy *was a mythical battle between gods and giants. In Greek, the word* gigas *means "giant." According to legend, the gods fought off the giants when they attacked the Acropolis, Athen's sacred fortress.*

This mythical battle between Greek gods and giants was called a *gigantomachy*. The principal magistrates of Athens, or *archons*, were responsible for the organization of the festivities. Ten other magistrates took charge of the sacrifices.

Musical contests, athletic competitions, and horse races were held several days before the great Panathenaean procession. Winners received large vases filled with oil made from the city-state's sacred olive trees.

On the last day of the festival the colorful procession gathered at the Dipylon Gate. The people of Athens lined the streets to watch the parade of horsemen, athletic champions, magistrates, Athenian wise men, Athena's trusted treasurers, ergastinae, and sacrificial cows and rams. The procession climbed the Acropolis and presented the golden peplos to Athena.

workers. These women had the honor of weaving a sacred saffron-colored peplos to honor Athena. On the ceremonial garment they wove a design showing giants in battle against the gods.

A Famous Frieze

The Panathenaean procession was a frieze sculpted in a band around the walls of the Parthenon, a magnificent temple to Athena on the Acropolis.

THE RIGHTS OF THE CITIZEN

Every Greek belonged to a specific city-state that functioned like a small, independent country with its own territory, beliefs, and customs. City-states such as Athens, Sparta, Corinth, and Thebes had their own laws, courts, coins, and measurements for weight and distance. Each celebrated different heroes and had its own calendar based on religious holidays.

ATHENIAN BORN

Except in rare cases, it was not possible to become Athenian. A person had to be born Athenian. Up until 451 B.C., a child whose father was an Athenian citizen was considered to be a citizen of Athens even if his

Owls

Coins in Athens were engraved with pictures of owls. The owl was the symbolic animal of the goddess Athena.

Slaves who fought bravely on the battlefield became free men and were granted full Athenian citizenship. It was much rarer for individuals to receive naturalization.

A Spartan could lose his political rights if he didn't join in a ritual group meal called

or her mother was foreign born. After 451 B.C. the laws became more strict. In order to be regarded as Athenian, both of the child's parents had to be from Athens. The laws were just as strict in Sparta.

However, under certain conditions, groups of men could receive the right to call themselves Athenian citizens. In 406 B.C., Athens conquered Sparta at the Battle of Arginusae.

a *syssition* that was part of a young man's military training. Theban citizens could be stripped of their citizenship, too, if they practiced certain crafts or trades.

In Athens a citizen who neglected to take care of an aging parent, who was lazy, who gave false witness, who dishonored a judge, or who deserted the army could lose the rights of a citizen.

SECOND-CLASS CITIZENS

In Athens, foreigners could obtain residency. Within one month of their arrival in the city-state, they had to register as a *metic*. Metics were free men who didn't have the same rights as citizens. They paid special, relatively low taxes called *metoikon,* but they weren't allowed to own land or houses. Even if they married Athenian women, their children would never become Athenian citizens.

But metics were free to live where they pleased and to speak in public. In the army they served as foot soldiers or as seamen. They could receive honors, titles, and the right to own property for services performed for the city-state. On rare occasions metic soldiers were even rewarded with Athenian citizenship.

Metics practiced many crafts and trades. They worked as bakers and hairdressers, for example. Some of them even became doctors and bankers.

Women's Rights

Greek women were not citizens in the same way that Greek men were. They were excluded from the political life of their city-state. They did, though, pass on citizenship to their sons.

In the Case of a Metic

If a citizen murdered a metic, his action was considered "involuntary," and he could not be put to death. If a metic killed someone, though, his trial was held in a separate court where sentences tended to be much more harsh.

sold for 1,000 drachmas or more. At this time, skilled laborers working on the large construction site at the Athenian Acropolis earned only one drachma for a full day's work.

A SLAVE'S LIFE

Slaves were men and women who had no rights at all. They had no freedom, no family, and no personal belongings. A child born to slave parents would live a slave's life. Masters had the power of life and death over slaves, and only masters could decide whether or not slaves should be freed. Freed slaves would have a political status similar to that of the metics, but they would continue to serve their former masters as well.

Some slaves were Greek citizens who had been taken prisoner in war. Others were free men who, unable to pay back their debts, had sold themselves as slaves to their creditors.

Most slaves, though, were bought and sold, and they were very expensive to buy. In 434 B.C., for example, the lowest price for a slave was 178 drachmas. "Special" slaves such as doctors were more valuable and could be

THE POPULATION OF ATHENS

Athens and its surrounding territories were highly populated in comparison with outlying regions. There were approximately forty-five inhabitants per square mile (about seventeen people per square kilometer). In poorer regions such as Phocaia or Arcadia, there were only thirteen inhabitants per square mile (about five per square kilometer).

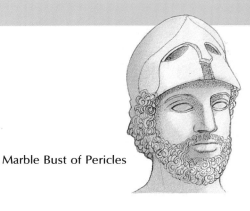

Marble Bust of Pericles

Around 432 B.C. the population of Athens broke down like this:

Citizens	35,000–45,000
Citizens and their families	110,000–150,000
Metics	10,000–15,000
Metics and their families	25,000–40,000
Slaves	80,000–115,000

school district. Once this system was established, children added the name of their deme to the name they inherited from their father. For example, Pericles was "son of Zanthippus from the deme of Chosarges."

Demes were grouped together into ten tribes. Each tribe contained an equal number of citizens. Every young Athenian citizen had a chance of becoming head of his city-state.

THE STIRRINGS OF DEMOCRACY

An Athenian statesman named Cleisthenes introduced the concept of democracy to Athens in 509 B.C. He divided Athenian citizens into *demes*, or small communities. Greeks belonged to their deme as we belong to a

Democracy means "people power" and comes from the Greek word demos, which means "people." In reality, though, citizens did not make up the majority of the Athenian population. Citizens would never have been able to devote all their time and energy to politics if it had not been for the many slaves and metics who ensured the city-state's economic welfare and built all of its public works. But metics, slaves, and women were excluded from the democratic process.

Although Athenian democracy expressed the will of a select group of people, it was an enormous step to allow all citizens to participate in a democratic government. It was here in Athens that the principle of rule by the people first took hold.

THE CROWDED PLACE

The citizens came together to participate in the decisions made by the people's assembly, or ecclesia. Because there were many participants, the seat of this assembly was called the *Pnyx*, which meant "the crowded place."

Sometimes the Athenian citizens' enthusiasm waned, and they didn't bother to participate in the ecclesia's decisions. When this happened, Scythian archers, who made up the Athenian police force, blocked the city streets and rounded up the lazy citizens with ropes dipped in bright red powder. People were embarrassed to appear at the Pynx in clothing stained with red marks!

Before the beginning of each session, pigs were sacrificed to the gods, and priests traced a sacred circle around the assembly with the animals' blood. It was thought that if the gods favored the ecclesia, the people would not be misled.

Orators spoke one after another, and the meetings often lasted a long time. Food and drink were served to the statesmen.

Assembly participants eventually became so numerous that Cleisthenes had to introduce a restricted council called the *bouleuterion*. Each tribe sent fifty citizens to sit on

The Courts

Cases involving murder were decided by a court of justice called the Areopagus, *which sat on a hill just outside the city. The name Areopagus came from Ares, the god of war, who was believed to have stood trial for murder on this same hill. All other cases were tried in the* Helilea, *the large, open-air court in Athens' city center. It was named after the Greek word for sun,* helios.

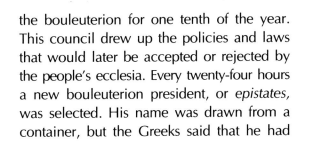

the bouleuterion for one tenth of the year. This council drew up the policies and laws that would later be accepted or rejected by the people's ecclesia. Every twenty-four hours a new bouleuterion president, or *epistates*, was selected. His name was drawn from a container, but the Greeks said that he had

been chosen by the gods. Such drawings meant that every citizen had at least one chance to hold the city's seal and take responsibility for the running of the state.

LIMITED POWER

Each magistrate was elected for one year by a show of hands in the ecclesia. Pericles was so popular that he was reelected *strategos*, or military commander, thirty times in a row.

Before assuming their new roles, magistrates had to pass an exam called the *docimasia*, which tested their morality and political capabilities. Once magistrates were sworn into office, they had to account for all their actions.

The assembly could vote to "ostracize" statesmen suspected of political ambition. Ostracism was the assembly's way of removing unpopular politicians, and often this led to ten years of exile. The names of banished citizens were written on stones, shells, or broken pieces of pottery called *ostrakons*. Condemned citizens were not given the chance to justify themselves.

In 484 B.C. an Athenian statesman named Aristides was accused by a citizen who could neither read nor write. Aristides himself wrote his name on the stone that banished him into exile.

A WORLD AT WAR

"**P**olemos reigns over the world," said a philosopher living at the beginning of the fifth century B.C. This sad statement underlines the importance of war in ancient times. Polemos was not a king; it was the name Greeks gave to war.

Greeks sometimes joined forces in fighting against threats by their common enemy the "barbarians." When the great Persian king Darius and his successor Xerxes tried to take over Greece, the Greeks stood up against them. After the Greek victory at the Battle of Plataea in 479 B.C., there was no further risk of Persian invasion.

However, Greeks often fought among themselves as well. The more powerful city-states such as Athens dominated the others. Those who resisted a takeover were destroyed, and their populations were subjected to the tragic fate of the conquered. Athenians killed all the men on the Cycladian island of Melos, for example, and turned the women and children into slaves. The people of Melos were Greek, but the city-state had made the mistake of trying to resist Athenian rule.

ring period began in 431 B.C. with the outbreak of the Peloponnesian War between Athens and Sparta. This war would involve all of Greece for the next twenty-seven years. A league of city-states on the Peloponnesus backed Sparta, while Athens' allies joined to form the Delian league.

A peace treaty was signed in 421 B.C. after a plague devastated the Athenian population. But hostilities broke out once more, and the evenly matched enemies continued to battle for many years to come.

During the course of a 150-year period, Athens was at war with other city-states an average of two years out of three. This war-

Athens the Warrior

Throughout a century and a half, Athens battled with the other city-states on an average of two years out of three. The Peloponnesian War alone lasted twenty-seven years.

Terrible Medusa

Soldiers' breastplates, or cuirasses, were quite often decorated with the head of Medusa, a terrible mythical monster with snakes for hair. Such frightening designs were intended to protect the warrior and scare the enemy.

These wars marked the beginning of the end for the newborn Athenian democratic state. In time, all of Greece would be torn apart, never to recover.

A SOLDIER'S LIFE

Serving as a soldier was not a profession; it was an obligation. All Greek citizens were soldiers. In Sparta, boys' education was almost entirely devoted to military training. There was no greater glory than to give one's life in defense of the city-state.

"Passerby, go and tell the people of Sparta that we died here to defend Spartan laws." These words were engraved on the tomb of King Leonidas and the three hundred Spartans who died to keep the Persians from getting through the narrow mountain pass at Thermopylae in 480 B.C..

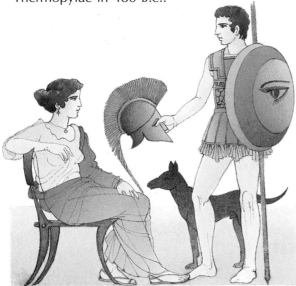

When Athenian men turned eighteen, they became *ephebos*. This meant that they had to undergo two years of military training. They could be called into military service from the moment they finished their training until the age of sixty!

A soldier's means of transportation was not a question of taste or personal choice, but rather one of money. Soldiers from the city-state's wealthiest families served in the cavalry because they were the only ones who could afford to raise and keep horses. These cavalrymen rode without saddles or stirrups.

Hoplites, or armed foot soldiers, also needed a decent income to purchase a complete set of armor. This included a helmet, a shield, a spear, and a sword.

Hoplites' helmets were made of bronze and were lined with leather or felt to protect the soldier's head. They were decorated with high crests made of horse hair. The height of the helmet increased along with the rank of its wearer.

Corinthian helmets covered the warrior's whole face and included nose pieces and fixed face gear. When the warrior wasn't fighting, he pushed his helmet back on top of his head. Athenian helmets didn't have nose pieces, but the movable face gear could be removed as needed.

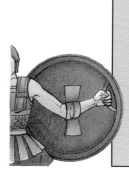

Hoplites' Shields

There were two attachments inside each soldier's shield. The soldier passed his left arm through the one in the middle, which was shaped like an armband. He then grasped the other one, at the edge of the shield, with his hand.

The shields were often decorated with illustrations of the Medusa's head (a mythical monster who had snakes for hair), but other emblems, especially animals' heads, were also used. Emblems on shields were thought to have magical powers and were designed to guard against bad luck.

The hoplite's cuirass, the piece of armor covering the back and breast, was made of bronze and fit snugly to the body. Hoplites also wore leather cuirasses reinforced with thin, metal plates and several layers of leather.

Their round shields were made of wood and covered with leather, animal skin, or bronze. When hoplites were not fighting, they turned their shields over to slaves because they didn't want to wear themselves out carrying the heavy equipment.

THE BATTLEFIELD

On the battlefield, hoplites fought in closed, organized formations known as *phalanxes*. They lined up shoulder to shoulder to form long blocks of men that were eight to twelve rows deep. Each hoplite's shield protected the right side of the man standing next to him.

Poor citizens who couldn't afford to buy expensive hoplite armor served as archers,

stone slingers, and javelin throwers. Their role was to harass the enemy. They also worked as oarsmen on long, narrow, three-story ships known as *triremes*. Flute music helped them to row in unison. Sometimes they broke into rhythmic chant and shouted war songs together.

Triremes, boats 135 feet (41 meters) long and 20 feet (6 meters) wide, carried crews of up to two hundred rowers. The hundreds of oars moved the boats smoothly and swiftly over the water. Their bronze tips, which were used to damage enemy ships, made them seem like nautical swords.

A common military tactic was for several triremes to close in on an enemy ship until it had no room to maneuver. When the enemy ship was trapped, the triremes rammed it with their front ends, smashing it to pieces.

THE PANHELLENIC GAMES

Greeks were often at war, but when they arrived at the shrines where the Panhellenic Games were played, they quickly forgot their quarrels. These "all-Greek" games were open to athletes from every city-state who were free men. Slaves and foreigners didn't have the right to compete but were welcome to attend as spectators. Women were absolutely forbidden to attend the games. Those who tried to see the competition were subject to the death penalty!

Swift and Strong

The armed sprint was a test of a soldier's endurance. Each young man had to run roughly 437 yards (400 meters) weighted down by helmet and shield.

Greek games took place at four different shrines. Those games that honored the god Zeus took place at Olympia and Nemea; those celebrating Poseidon were played at Isthmia in Corinth; and Apollo's games were held at Delphi. The Olympic, Nemean, Isthmian, and Pythian (Delphi) games each took place once every four years. Every twelve months, games would be held at a different shrine. This meant that there were Panhellenic celebrations every year.

It was not easy for Greek athletes and spectators to know when the games were held because each city-state had its own calendar. This made it very difficult to announce a starting date that everybody would understand. The start of the games at Delphi was announced six months in advance by representatives who traveled throughout the Greek empire inviting athletes from very city-state.

The Olympic Games went on for a week. Religious ceremonies and sacrifices to Zeus took place the first day, while the procession and victory banquet for winning athletes were held on closing day. That left five days for athletic competition. In the fifth century B.C., there were eight Olympic events for adults and three for children.

The race around one length of the track: Adults and children

The race around two lengths of the track: Adults

Wrestling: Adults and children

Boxing: Adults and children

Pankration (boxing and wrestling): Adults

Farther than Today

To throw the javelin, athletes often placed two fingers through a leather strap wrapped around the javelin's shaft. This position, which allowed them to rotate the javelin as they released it, enabled them to increase the distance of their throw.

Pentathlon (long jump, discus and javelin throwing, running, wrestling): Adults

Four-horse chariot races: Adults

Horse racing: Adults

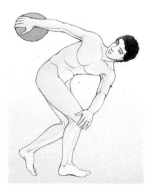

Olympic champions were rewarded with simple crowns made of leaves. In Olympia, children presented wreaths of olive leaves to winning athletes; in Nemea, winners received crowns of parsley. The true prize was the honor and glory bestowed upon the successful competitor.

Athletes caught cheating were subjected to heavy fines. In Olympia, excavators have dug up bases of bronze statues honoring Zeus called Zanes that were built with the money earned from such fines.

RUNNERS

Greeks did not run 26-mile (42-kilometer) marathons. Athletes never ran more than 3 miles (4.8 kilometers) in competition. *Marathon* was a plain, not far from Athens, where the Athenians won a great victory over the Persians when they tried to invade Greece.

In September of 490 B.C. Greeks clashed with Persians on the Marathon plain. After a fierce battle, the city-state warriors were victorious. More than six thousand Persians were killed. The tactics of the Greek military commander Miltiades were so clever that only 192 Greeks died. They were buried on the battlefield under a burial mound, or *tumulus,* that can still be seen today.

One Greek soldier was sent to inform Athens of the glorious victory. In his haste to share the good news with his fellow citizens as soon as possible, the messenger ran the twenty-six miles to Athens as fast as he could. Upon reaching the town center he cried out, "Rejoice, we are victorious!" and then collapsed from exhaustion. Today, athletes run marathons to commemorate this legendary victory.

Greek athletes preferred sprints at Delphi to those at Olympia, Athens, or Epidaurus because the track at Delphi was shorter. According to tradition, it was the hero Heracles who had determined that tracks should be 600 feet (183 meters) long. However, because each city-state had its own system of measurement, feet were not the same length everywhere. An Olympic foot was 12.16 inches (32 centimeters) long, whereas a Delphic foot had only 11.5 inches (30 centimeters). This meant that a 600-foot track was actually 630.6 feet long (192.3 meters) in Olympia, 606.6 feet (185 meters) in Athens, 594.6 feet (181.3) in Epidaurus, and 582.5 (177.6) in Delphi.

For the Greeks, the word *stadium* did not refer to a place. Rather, it was a six-hundred-foot unit of measurement. To "run the stadium race" was to run one length of the track. This race was not only the fastest and shortest, it was also the oldest and therefore the most important. It was run at the first Olympic games, which were held in 776 B.C. The winner of the stadium race received the distinguished honor of giving his name to the four-year period, or *Olympiad,* that followed his victory.

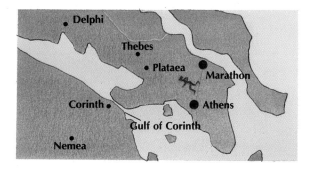

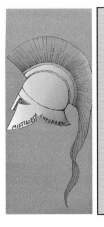

Miltiades' Helmet

After the victory at Marathon, Miltiades dedicated his bronze helmet to Zeus, the master of all gods, whose shrine was at Olympia. On the side of the helmet, Greek letters can still be read — spelling out the name of the famous Athenian commander.

TRAINING

Athletes trained in gymnasiums. These athletic centers were composed of an open-air track and a covered gallery that protected athletes from the rain and bright sun. Athletes trained in the nude. The word *gymnasium* was related to the Greek adjective *gymnos,* meaning "nude."

Before exercising, athletes applied oil to their bodies to loosen up their muscles. When they were done practicing, they removed oil, sweat, and dust with a metal scraper called a *strigil* before washing up. Every athlete carried with him a strigil, a sponge, and a small flask of perfume to refresh his body

after the workout. There were always dressing rooms, baths, and lounges near sports facilities.

FEMALE COMPETITORS

Every four years girls participated in their own games in honor of the goddess Hera, Zeus' wife. Girls who ran the 35-yard (32-meter) dash were divided into three age groups: children, adolescents, and young women. Winners were given the right to eat some of the cow sacrificed to Hera.

However, it was only Spartan girls whose training was as serious as that of boys. The Spartan girls' athletic activities offended other Greeks who found them lacking in feminine modesty. They were jeeringly called *phainomeridae,* or "those who dared to reveal their thighs!"

LONG JUMPING

Greeks used hand-held throwing weights for long jumping. The athlete ran with a weight in each hand, and when he jumped, he reached forward with both arms. The weights pulled him forward. Just before his feet touched the ground, he threw his arms backward and released the weights. This method allowed him to jump much farther than today's athletes.

These weights were made of stone or lead. They were round and had a hole in the middle where athletes could insert their fingers to get a firm grip.

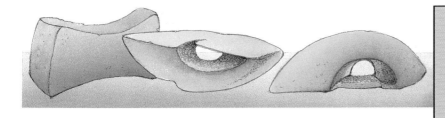

CONTACT SPORTS

When wrestlers wanted to surrender, they raised their index or middle finger. To win an upright wrestling match, wrestlers had to throw their opponent to the ground three times.

Greek athletes also boxed. They wrapped leather straps dipped in oil or grease around their fingers, palms, and wrists to protect their hands. Boxers' blows could be aimed only at an opponent's face.

The most violent contact sport was the *pankration,* a mixture of wrestling and boxing. This was a favorite spectator sport because athletes could do almost anything to get their opponent to surrender. Only biting and eye gouging were forbidden. If an athlete tried to cheat, the referee hit him with a stick.

GREEK THEATER

Tragedy and comedy were born in ancient Greece. And several of the works written by the great Greek playwrights more than 2,500 years ago are still performed in our theaters today.

Dramatic presentations first appeared as part of the celebrations honoring Dionysus. During the festivities, hymns praising Dionysus were sung throughout the processions and dances. *Dithyrambs,* as these hymns in verse were called, were sung in dialogues between dramatic characters and a chorus. These hymns were the beginning of modern theater.

The first playgoers sat on simple wooden platforms that were set up before each performance. Open-air theaters were not built until later. These were permanent wooden bleachers built into a hillside that sloped down to a round stage below. The circular stage, called the *orchestra,* was where the chorus danced and sang. In the center of this stage was an altar dedicated to Dionysus.

The chorus entered and exited through side corridors called *paradoi.* The actors came in and out through doors in the back wall of the stage, or *skene,* which was painted to look like the play's setting. Our word *scenery* comes from the Greek word *skene.* Stone theaters such as the famous theater at Epidaurus, weren't built until the fourth century B.C.

Stage equipment was simple. There were rough pieces of painted scenery that turned on axles. A crane and cables in the theater's rafters allowed characters playing the roles of gods to swing across the sky. Murders were never presented on stage, but a special platform allowed bodies killed offstage to be rolled out in full view of the audience.

Female Roles

There were no actresses in Greek drama. All of the characters, including the female roles, were played by men — dressed up to look like women.

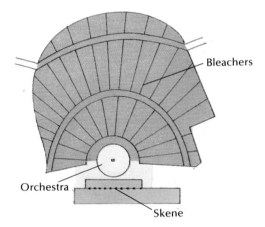

Bleachers

Orchestra

Skene

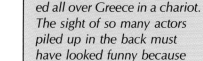

A Strange Chariot

Thespis and his troupe traveled all over Greece in a chariot. The sight of so many actors piled up in the back must have looked funny because there were a lot of jokes about Thespis's chariot.

THE FIRST TRAGIC HERO

In the sixth century B.C., Thespis decided to enliven the dialogue sung by the chorus because he thought most dithyrambs were dull. In 534 B.C. his first tragedy—perhaps the world's first tragedy—was performed at the new theater built to honor Dionysus on the south side of the Athenian Acropolis.

It was Thespis who created the tragic hero. This was a person who appeared on stage to enact the most dramatic moment in his life. The hero's moral conflict was explained by the chorus, which served as an intermediary, or link, between the hero and the audience.

The tragic heroes on the Greek stage were often characters that had first appeared in Homer's epics, or long narrative poems. Epic

poems, however, required the listener or reader to imagine how the hero and his surroundings looked. Tragedies brought the hero's dilemma to life.

ATHENS, CITY OF TRAGEDY

Dionysus was the god of theater, and Athens was the city of tragedy. Every year, two important Dionysian festivals were held in Athens: the Great Dionysia and the Lenaea. The celebrations included contests for the best tragedy and the best comedy.

Dithyramb and comedy competitions were held during the first three days of the Great Dionysia, while the contest for the best tragedy took place at the end of the festival. Each contestant was required to enter three tragedies and one *satyr* play, which was a comic skit about a Greek myth.

Festivals in honor of Dionysus were national celebrations to which everybody was invited. In Pericles's time, poor citizens who had to stop working to come to the theater were given a small sum to make up for lost wages.

Such benefits attracted many spectators to the performances. The theaters in Athens and Epidaurus, for example, could each hold 15,000 people. The theater in Argos seated 20,000.

The only reserved seats in the house were the chairs with backs in the first row. These

The Choregoi

Wealthy citizens who financed the theatrical competitions were called choregoi. *How pleased they were if the chorus they had sponsored won the competition!*

When Lysictatis' choir won, he built a grand monument. Other choregoi had bronze stands erected in the street.

privileged spots were saved for priests and magistrates. The great priest of Dionysus sat in the front row directly in front of the altar. Citizens and foreigners sat in the upper levels. Women were seated in the very back of the theater with the slaves.

Despite these regulations, there were many disputes about who should sit where. Special theater police who carried sticks often had to settle arguments between spectators.

During the Great Dionysia, Athenians watched four or five plays in a row. This meant that they listened to more than 20,000 lines of verse in one sitting. Moreover, many people came back to the theater several days in a row. They ate and drank in their seats. *Choregoi,* the financial backers of the spectacles, had cakes and wine distributed throughout the audience.

THE LEGACY OF THE THEATER

These gifted Greek playwrights were inspired to write many plays. Unfortunately, though, most Greek tragedies were performed just once onstage and were never written down. Only about thirty-five of the thousand or so tragedies that were presented in ancient Greece have survived.

We know only seven of the twenty-four tragedies written by Aeschylus. He lived during the Greek and Persian wars (525–456 B.C.). Among the plays he left us are *The Persians, Seven Against Thebes,* and *Oresteia.*

Sophocles (495–406 B.C.) is known for having introduced the presence of a third actor into the plot of Greek plays. His dramas sing the praises of the solitary hero. Many of his tragedies, such as *Antigone, Ajax, Electra,* and *Oedipus,* are performed in theaters today.

Euripides (480–406 B.C.) is known for the innovations he brought to tragedy. He was interested in exploring the psychology of his characters, and it was he who decided that the chorus should be independent of the play's action. His plays *Medea,* Andromache, and *Iphigenia* reflect the grim atmosphere in Greece during the Peloponnesian War at the end of the fifth century B.C. His work influenced the seventeenth-century French tragedians Racine and Corneille.

Sophocles   Euripides

IN THE LAND OF THE GODS

The Greeks believed that a whole population of divine beings oversaw all that went on in the worlds of the living and the dead. These gods had both supernatural powers and human weaknesses. They were born; they fell in love; they got angry and jealous, and they lied; they married and had children; and sometimes they even died. The stories of these gods created a giant picture of the Greek world and the nature of its inhabitants. Through them, the Greeks passed on knowledge from generation to generation about who they were and how their world was ordered.

Not all Greek gods were pleasant to look at. Some of them were ugly and deformed. Hephaestus, the god of blacksmiths, walked with a limp. He was injured when he tried to defend his mother Hera from his father Zeus. Zeus threw him down from the top of Mount Olympus. He fell for an entire day, and when evening came, he crashed to earth on the isle of Lemnos.

Pan, the god of shepherds, was half animal and half man; he had a hairy body and the legs of a goat. He frightened his mother the day he was born. His helpful father carried him to Olympus, where the child entertained the gods. They named him Pan, the greek word for "all," because he delighted them all.

Other gods, however, possessed supernatural beauty. Among the most famous were Apollo, tall and well built with long, dark curls; Athena, the proud goddess with blue-green eyes; and Aurora, the goddess of dawn, whose fingers were the color of roses.

THE BIRTH OF THE GODS

As the story goes, in the beginning, Gaea, the earth, was born of Chaos and gave birth to Uranos, the sky and the mountains. Uranos was Gaea's equal because the sky covered the earth. Uranos and Gaea gave birth to the first divine generation. This included

the one-eyed Cyclopes; the Hecatonchires, which were monsters with one hundred hands; and the Titans.

Uranos couldn't bear the sight of his ugly children, so he forced them to live without light in the belly of their mother, the earth. Gaea managed to have her children freed and demanded that they get revenge for her. Cronus, the youngest Titan and the god of time, wounded his father with his scythe and claimed victory over him.

Cronus and his sister Rhea gave birth to the second divine generation, which included the great Olympians. Gaea and Uranos, who could see into the future, warned Cronus that one of his sons would eventually dethrone him. This prediction led Cronus to eat all his children the day they were born.

Rhea, who was very upset by this, decided to protect her sixth child. When Rhea's son Zeus was born in the middle of the night, she told nobody. The next morning, she presented her husband with a bundle of blankets wrapped around a stone.

Cronus gobbled up the blankets without noticing that there was no baby inside. Young

Zeus was raised on milk from his pet goat Amalthaea and the honey from the bees. When he grew up, he tricked his father into taking a drug that would return all the swallowed children to life. When Demeter, Hera, Hades, and Poseidon came back to life, they

helped their younger brother defeat Cronus and the Titans. After a battle that lasted for ten years, called the Gigantomachy, the great Olympians succeeded in chasing the Titans from the heavens. They drew lots to decide who would govern the different parts of the world. Zeus became the god of the heavens, Poseidon became the god of the sea, and Hades became the lord of the underworld.

The Greeks believed that the gods lived on Mount Olympus. They were protected from the sight of men by what Homer called "the great gate of clouds."

The ancients believed that the gods made their presence known to people through signs, such as the rustling of the leaves and the roaring of thunder. In sacred places where the gods had "appeared," the Greeks built sanctuaries and temples to shelter the gods from the elements.

THE FAMILY OF GODS

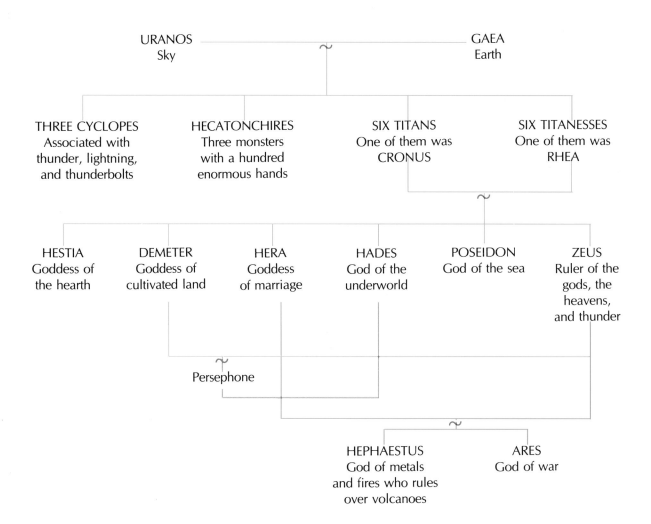

Here are a few of the myths about the great gods. The following story explains the cycle of the seasons.

Persephone and her friends were picking flowers when Hades kidnapped her and led her to the underworld. Her mother Demeter traveled around the world to find her. On the tenth day of her journey, the all-seeing sun revealed the kidnapper's name. Zeus ordered Hades to return Persephone. But the young girl could not return to the world of the living because she had eaten a pomegranate seed. Zeus suggested that Persephone divide her time between her mother and her husband.

So, in springtime, Persephone sprouted from

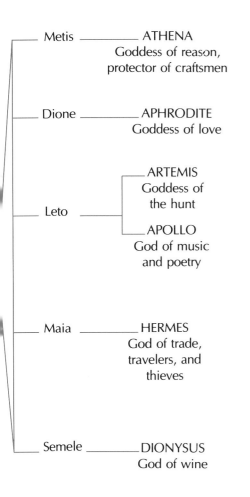

Metis —————— ATHENA
Goddess of reason,
protector of craftsmen

Dione —————— APHRODITE
Goddess of love

ARTEMIS
Goddess of
the hunt
Leto
APOLLO
God of music
and poetry

Maia —————— HERMES
God of trade,
travelers, and
thieves

Semele ————— DIONYSUS
God of wine

the flesh of his own thigh until the time came for the child to be born. Three months later he gave birth to Dionysus.

Zeus knew that after his daughter's birth, the goddess of prudence, Metis, would give him a son who would dethrone him. To avoid this fate, he swallowed Metis before his daughter Athena was born. He asked Hephaestus to split his skull open. When he did, Athena sprang from her father's head in full armor.

Apollo and Artemis were twins. Both of them were archers, and they shot arrows that caused rapid death to humans. The day they were born, their mother Leto suffered Hera's wrath. Hera was furious to discover that her husband had been unfaithful to her. Leto became a homeless wanderer who searched desperately for a place where she could give birth to her children.

The earth feared Hera and so refused to take Leto in. Only one barren rock agreed to accept her. In gratitude, Apollo made the small rocky island in the Aegean Sea the very center of the Greek world. He named it Delos, which meant "the heaven-built island." This was the story of how the land of Greece came into being.

the earth like a new shoot of grass. In winter, the ground was barren because she had returned to the dark underworld.

Dionysus, the god of the vine, was born twice. His mother Semele had been foolish enough to ask Zeus to appear in all his splendor. When the god appeared, she was struck dead by a thunderbolt. Zeus saved the child by sewing him into

FIND OUT MORE

Coolidge, Oliver. *Golden Days of Greece*. New York: Harper Junior Books, 1990.

Green, Roger L. *Tales of Greek Heroes*. New York: Penguin, 1974.

Odijk, Pamela. *The Greeks*. Englewood Cliffs, New Jersey: Silver Burdett, 1989.

Peach, Susan and Millard, Anne. *The Greeks*. Tulsa, Oklahoma: EDC Publishing, 1990.

Powell, Anton. *Ancient Greece* (Cultural Atlas for Young People). New York: Facts on File, 1989.

Powell, Anton. *Greece*. New York: Franklin Watts, 1987.

Rutland, Jonathan. *An Ancient Greek Town*. New York: Franklin Watts, 1986.

GLOSSARY

Acropolis. A fortified area built on a hill at the center of a town. The acropolis in Athens was the most famous one.

Andron. The dining room reserved for the men of the house.

Aule. The living room or hall.

Bouleuterion. A council of the people that was limited to a select number.

Chiton. A pleated women's tunic that fastened at the shoulders.

Chlamys. A short cloak worn by a man.

City-state. An independent community composed of a town and the surrounding countryside.

Clepsydra. A water clock, an instrument that tells time by measuring the flow of a quantity of water.

Delian League. The modern name for the alliance of city-states that joined with Athens in 477 B.C. to fight Sparta.

Deme. The community, or district, to which an Athenian citizen belonged.

Democratia. Democracy, or rule by the people.

Dithyramb. A hymn in praise of Dionysus; the first trace of modern theater.

Docimasia. The examination that a magistrate had to pass before he could assume his responsibilities.

Ecclesia. The people's assembly in Athens.

Epistates. The president of the bouleuterion. (See **bouleuterion.**)

Grammatist. A reading and writing teacher.

Gigantomachy. A mythical battle between gods and giants.

Gymnasium. The place where athletes trained.

Gynaceum. The section of the house reserved for the women.

Himation. A wool cloak worn by men and women.

Hoplite. An armed foot soldier.

Linear B. The writing used by the Mycenaeans, a people who lived on mainland Greece from 1600–1100 B.C.

Loutrophorus. A special vase used to hold the sacred water in which an Athenian girl bathed on the day before her wedding.

Marathon. The plain where the Greeks were victorious against the Persians; the name for a long-distance run in memory of this victory.

Metic. A foreigner who lived in Athens.

Oikos. The family dining room.

Ostracism. The system of voting out a politician and sending him into exile.

Paidotribe. An athletics coach.

Phalanx. The battle formation of the hoplites.

Philosopher. A Greek word meaning "lover of knowledge"; a scholar who tries to understand the meaning of the universe and the nature of human beings.

Pnyx. The place where the people's assembly met in Athens.

Polemus. The Greek word for war.

Panathenaea. An important holiday held every fourth year in honor of Athena.

Peplos. A tunic, the standard garment made from a rectangle of cloth.

Satyr. A short comic skit that made fun of a Greek myth.

Strategos. An Athenian military leader.

Stylus. A wooden writing instrument.

Symposium. The part of a banquet reserved for drinking.

Syssition. A ritual group meal that was part of a Spartan's military training.

Trireme. A long warship propelled by oars. Its main weapon was its pointed bow, which it used to ram enemy ships.

INDEX